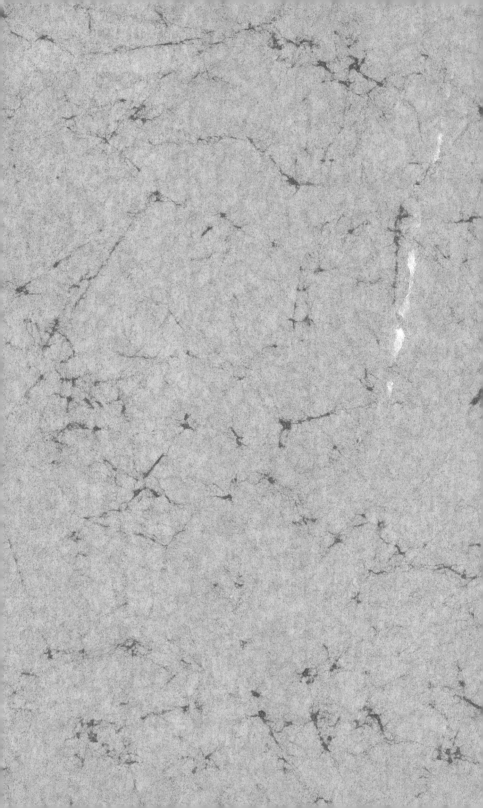

Eyewitness Accounts of the American Revolution

# The Battle
# of Brandywine
# Joseph Townsend

The New York Times & Arno Press

# PROCEEDINGS

### OF

# THE HISTORICAL SOCIETY

### OF PENNSYLVANIA.

Vol. I.    SEPTEMBER, 1846.    No. 7.

*Stated Meeting of Council; June 23, 1846.*

VICE PRESIDENT ELWYN in the Chair,

Mr. Desmond offered a letter from the New York Historical Society, with a memorial to be laid before Congress, asking that the intention to lay a duty upon books be relinquished.

Mr. Desmond moved that the subject be referred to a committee of three, which motion was carried, and the chairman appointed as the committee, Messrs. Desmond, Duane, and Lewis.

On motion of Dr. Coates it was resolved, that Mr. Rawle be appointed a committee to prepare an obituary notice of Mr. Redmond Conyngham, our lately deceased member.

The following gentlemen were elected contributing members: The Right Rev. Dr. Alonzo Potter, Dr. William Shippen. As an honorary member, Professor Schele De Vere, of the University of Virginia.

#### DONATIONS.

*From S. Salisbury.* The catalogue of the Pennsylvania State Library.

*From Simon Stevens.* The Bloody Buoy.

*From Miss. Heckewelder.* Sundry pamphlets and papers.*

*From Charles C. Ashmead.* A fac simile of the medal given to General Armstrong for his plan of attack against Kittaning, in 1758.

*From Col. Richard M. Crain, of Harrisburg.* Sundry interesting papers of ancient date.*

*From Sidney V. Smith.* Sundry Books.*

*From J. William Wallace.* The London Chronicle of 1758.

*From Mr. Duane.* Copy of the genealogical tree of William Penn's descendants.

*From Dr. Thaddeus N. Harris, of Cambridge.* MS. Journa of a voyage to Pennsylvania, in 1690.

* A list of these donations will be furnished in the next number.

# PLAN OF THE BATTLE GROUND.

The accompanying plan, of the battle ground of Brandywine, is from an actual survey made during the past summer, under the direction of John S. Bowen and J. Smith Futhey, Esquires, of West Chester. The position of the British and American forces, of many of the houses, and of the woods, as they existed, was ascertained and laid down from a rare and valuable map kindly loaned the committee by the Franklin Institute. As this map was published but a few months after the battle, and is (in the opinion of gentlemen familiar with the history and scene of the action) drawn with great accuracy, the committee have followed it implicitly. It bears the following title :

" Battle of Brandywine in which the rebels were defeated, September 11th, " 1777, by the army under the command of General Sir William Howe."

Note.—" The operations of the column under the command of his Excellency " Lieutenant General Knyphausen, is engraved from a plan drawn on the spot " by S. W. Werner, Lieutenant of Hessian Artillery, engraved by William Faden, " Charing Cross, 1778."

" Published according to Act of Parliament, by Willliam Faden, Charing " Cross, (London,) April, 1778."

The following references to the respective columns under the command of Lord Cornwallis and General Knyphausen, are copied from the British map.

*References to the column under the Command of Lieutenant General Earl Cornwallis.*

**A. A.** Column under the command of Lieutenant General Earl Cornwallis, after having crossed the forks of the Brandywine at 2 o'clock in the afternoon.

**B. B.** The third brigade, which was not brought into action, but kept in reserve in the rear of the fourth brigade.

**C.** Two squadrons of Dragoons which were not employed.

**D.** Light Infantry and Chasseurs beginning the attack.

**E. E.** Attack of the guards and Hessian Grenadiers who forced the enemy on the first onset.

**F.** A part of the enemy's right forced by the 2d Light Infantry and Chasseurs.

**G. G.** The 1st British Grenadiers, the Hessian Grenadiers and the guards entangled in the woods.

**H. H. H.** March of the 2d Light Infantry, 2d Grenadiers, and 4th Brigade beyond Dilworth, where they dislodged a corps of the enemy strongly posted.

*References to the column under the command of His Excellency Lieutenant General Knyphausen.*

**a. a.** Column under the command of His Excellency Lieutenant General Knyphausen in march at 9 in the morning, his van having drove back the rebel detachments which attempted to defend the defiles from Welchs' Tavern to the heights of Chadds' Ford.

**b. b.** Heights and woods occupied by the rebels. **c.** Small Fleche raised by do.

**d.** The British Riflemen posted behind a house and supported by 100 men of General Stirn's Brigade.

**e.** The Queen's Rangers pursuing the enemy dislodged from the woods, f.

**g.** Four pieces of cannon, with the 49th Regiment to support the attack of the advanced troops, and the 28th Regiment who crossed the valley, h, to get to the height, i, which the enemy abandoned at their approach as well as the Fleche, c.

k. March of the troops to take the position, n, which was done under the fire of cannon in l, and under that of the enemy in m, m.

n. n. n. n. Position of the column from half after ten in the morning till four in the afternoon, when General Howe made his attack on the other side of the Brandywine creek, near Dilworth. The position of the rebels was then in o. o. o. o.

p. March of the troops to the Ford under the fire of the cannon, g. The enemy fired from their batteries, m, m.

r. Ford where the troops crossed the creek and charged the enemy, who at first opposed them with some resolution, but soon gave way. The Riflemen and Queen's Rangers, with the 71st, the 4th, and the 5th followed by all the British Regiments, and by General Stirn's Brigade forced the enemy to abandon their Batteries, m. m. And after some resistance near the houses, s. s, to retire at t. t., from which position they fired upon the troops with four pieces of cannon. The rebels afterwards retreated to Chester, the night favoured their escape and saved them from pursuit. Lieutenant General Knyphausen's column having joined General Howe, remained in the position u. u.

*Reference showing the names of the occupunts of the houses in the vicinity of the battle at that time, and the names of the present occupants, (1846.)*

1. George Strode's, subsequently Philip Price's (now Jonathan Paxson's.)
2. ———— ————, (now Dr. A. L. Elwyn's.)
3. Richard Strode's (the portion now remaining is in the occupancy of his son Richard Strode.
4. Widow Susannah Davis's (not standing at present, the house built upon its site occupied by Aaron Sharpless.)
5. Mary, widow of *John* Davis's, once Amos Davis's. (not standing.)
6. Mary, widow of *James* Davis's, once Daniel Davis's, (now modernized and occupied by Hibbert Davis.)
7. William Jones's, (now Brinton Jones's, his grandson.)
8. Isaac Davis's, (now Abraham Darlington's.)
9. John Woodward's, (not standing.)
10. Richard Evanson's, (now Lewis Brinton's.)
11. House believed to have been occupied by J. Bolton, (not standing.)
12. Isaac Garrett's, (not standing.)
13. Abraham Darlington's, (now Clement Biddle's.)
14. John Bennett's, (not standing.)
15. Edward Brinton, Esqrs. (now Edward B. Darlington, his grandson's.)
16. George Brinton's, (now Ziba Darlington's. This house was built in 1704, by William Brinton, great grand father of present occupant.)
17. William Thatcher's, (now William Thatcher's.)
18. Israel Gilpin's—Howes' Head Quarters, (now George Gilpin's.)
19. John Henderson's (Harlan Webb now occupies a house built on or near the spot.)
20. Samuel Painter's, (now William Painter's.)
21. Gideon Gilpin's, La Fayette's Head Quarters, (now Wiliam Painter's.)
22. Benjamin Ring's, Washington's Head Quarters, (now Chalkley Harvey's )
23. William Harvey's, (not standing.)
24. Davis's Tavern, (now in ruins.)
25. John Chadd's, (still standing.)
26. Amos House's (not standing.)
27. George Martin's, (now Gideon Williamson's)
28. Smith shop, (not standing.)
29. The largest body of forest now remaining in the district.
30. Height where cannon were fired by Sir Wm. Howe.
* * Pits in which soldiers were buried.
I I Ravine in which Greene covered the retreat.
J Wistar's woods.      † Artillery.

# SOME ACCOUNT

OF THE

## BRITISH ARMY,

UNDER THE COMMAND OF GENERAL HOWE,

AND OF

## THE BATTLE OF BRANDYWINE,

ON

The Memorable September 11th, 1777,

AND

THE ADVENTURES OF THAT DAY, WHICH CAME TO THE KNOWLEDGE
AND OBSERVATION OF

## JOSEPH TOWNSEND,

LATE OF BALTIMORE, MD.

ACCOMPANIED BY

A NOTICE OF THE LIFE OF JOSEPH TOWNSEND, AND AN HISTORICAL
SKETCH OF THE BATTLE.

&c. &c.

PUBLISHED BY TOWNSEND WARD,
NO. 45 SOUTH FOURTH STREET, PHILADELPHIA.
Press of the Historical Society of Pennsylvania.
1 8 4 6.

The committee on the Bulletin desire to return their thanks to the Library Committee of the Franklin Institute, for their permission to use the "Plan of the Battle of Brandywine," the property of the Institute, and to the following gentleman of West Chester and its vicinity, for their valuable assistance in the preparation of this and the following number. To John S. Bowen, J. Smith Futhey, John Hickman, Jr., Joseph C. Strode, and Ziba Darlington, Esqs., and to Dr. William Darlington; also to Henry C. Townsend, Esq., of Philadelphia.

*Hall of the Historical Society,* ⎱
*October 14th,* 1846. ⎰

# A SKETCH OF THE BATTLE OF BRANDYWINE.*

### (*September* 11*th*, 1777.)

The campaign of 1777 was devoted by Sir William Howe and the forces under his command to obtaining possession of the city of Philadelphia.

The importance of this place in a military point of view has been questioned on both sides, and both Washington and Howe have been censured for their pertinacity. It will be well, therefore, before entering upon the particulars of the engagement which decided its fate, to present some of the most prominent reasons for thus estimating the importance of this city.

Philadelphia was at that time the largest city in the revolted provinces; it was the seat of the Continental Congress and the centre of the colonies. Although commanding a ready access to the sea, it was capable of being readily protected from the approach of a hostile fleet, and it lay in the heart of an open, extended country, rich, comparatively populous, and so far but little disturbed during the war. Hence it was the proper seat of that body which devised measures and provided means for carrying on the war.

The moral influence resulting from the position of Congress at this point was also great. All do not reason as Statesmen or Generals. Whilst the seat of Congress was secure, men were led to mock at the arms which could not penetrate to the headquarters of the infant nation.

But the winter following its capture, and the early part of the succeeding campaign, were seasons of gloom and apathy from North to South; while on the other hand, the British felt secure in their possession of the city, until France had signified her intention of lending the Americans a helping hand.

Another reason, of weight, with both parties, was the fact that this region, was, owing to its position and the peaceful disposition of much of its population, less affected by the yoke of Britain, and less influenced by the enthusiasm of the other colonies. In the possession of the British, this disaffection to the cause of the revolution would tend to strengthen their hold upon the country, whilst on the other hand but little positive injury was experienced from it to the side of the Whigs.

Influenced by such reasons, Sir William Howe made repeated efforts in the earlier part of the campaign to draw Gen. Wash-

*The committee are indebted for the above sketch, to the kindness of John S. Bowen, and J. Smith Futhey, Esqrs., of West Chester.

ington from his position in New Jersey, so as to bring on an engagement that might open him a way across that state. Failing
in this, his forces were withdrawn, and preparations made for em-
barking the troops. Their destination being uncertain, the continental forces occupied the ground thus abandoned, with a view
to defend any point upon the Hudson that might be attacked, and
to watch any other movements of the fleet.

The British embarked on the fifth of July, but did not leave
Sandy Hook until the twenty-third. On the thirtieth they reached
the capes of Delaware Bay. Here learning the obstructions that
had been placed in the river, they set sail for Chesapeake Bay,
which they entered about the middle of August, on the twenty-
fourth of which month they effected a landing at Turkey's Point,
near the head of Elk (now Elkton.)

On the twenty-seventh, the vanguard under Sir William Howe
proceeded to the head of Elk, and on the following day to Gray's
Hill, about two miles to the eastward.

At the head of the Elk was a quantity of public and private
stores, including a considerable supply of salt, of which Washington in his official letters says " Every attempt will be made to secure that." The value of this article during the war will be remembered. One bushel was a sufficient bribe to induce the attempt to capture Squire Cheyney, for the price of which a suit
was subsequently brought before the Squire himself.

The stores were mostly secured ; the large amount of valuable
property removed by the residents required almost all the teams
within reach, so that several thousand bushels of corn and oats
fell into the hands of the enemy.

Howe immediately issued a proclamation declaring that private
property should be respected, and strict order and discipline maintained, and offering pardon and protection to all who would submit to the authority of Britain.

Three brigades, composing the rear guard, under Gen. Knyphausen remained at the landing to cover the debarkation of the
stores and artillery, whilst one brigade under Gen. Grant, occupied a central position between Howe and Knyphausen. On the
first of September Gen. Knyphausen, crossed over to Cecil Court
House, whence he proceeded on the east side and joined the
forces under Howe on the third of the month. Gen. Grant remained at the head of Elk to maintain the communication with
the shipping.

As soon as Gen. Washington had learned the preparations for
departure made in New York by the British troops, he took position at Morristown, N. J., whence he could command the highland
passes on the Hudson and oppose any renewed attempt to cross
New Jersey towards Philadelphia:

The time consumed in the embarkation indicated a longer
voyage than the ascent of the Hudson. Accordingly, whilst prepara-

tions to receive the enemy on that river and to the eastward were not neglected, the completion of the fortifications upon the Delaware was hastened, and the militia of the lower counties of Pennsylvaia and the state of Delaware was assembled at Chester and Wilmington.

The departure of the fleet was the signal for the march of the American troops to the southward. Gen. Stephen, with his division and that of Gen. Lincoln proceeded to Chester, Gen. Lincoln having been ordered to join Gen. Schuyler in the North. The divisions of Generals Sullivan and Sterling, with that of Gen. Greene, (composed of the brigades of Muhlenberg and Weedon) slowly approached, accompanied by Gen. Washington in person. Morgan's and Bland's regiments of horse were with them. Gen. Nash received orders, upon receipt of intelligence of the fleet's being off the capes of the Chesapeake, to embark with Proctor's artillery for Chester.

On the twenty-fourth of August, Washington marched through Philadelphia, passing down Front street, and up Chestnut street, about seven in the morning, and proceeded without delay to Chester.

From this time Washington was incessantly engaged in thoroughly reconnoitering the country between Philadelphia and the Chesapeake.

The Delaware militia had been early posted at the head of Elk, and entrusted with the removal of the stores ; on the twenty-seventh of August about nine hundred Pennsylvania militia marched in that direction.

The cavalry were placed under the command of Count Pulaski ; the Marquis La Fayette now first entered, as a volunteer, the revolutionary service.

Washington mentions in his correspondence heavy rains upon the twenty-sixth of August, which injured the arms and ammunition, the last rain spoken of prior to the eleventh of September ; on the latter date, therefore, the waters of Brandywine creek must have been low, and the fords shallow, as is usually the case at that season.

From the first movements of the British in advance, active skirmishing, sometimes of considerable bodies, took place. On the twenty-eighth the Americans took between thirty and forty prisoners, and twelve deserters from the navy and eight from the army came into their camp. These stated the British forces to be in good health, but the horses as having suffered from the length of the voyage. On the twenty-ninth Capt. Lee took twenty-four prisoners.

On the third of September Cornwallis, now joined by Knyphausen, moved forward and encamped above Pencader. A severe though brief encounter occurred between his division and Maxwell's regiment of foot. The British stated their loss at three killed and nineteen wounded, and that of the Americans at forty killed and wounded; but while the loss of the latter seems to be correctly given, it would appear that that of the former was much greater. A woman who came from their camp the next day, said that she had seen nine wagon loads of wounded brought in. Maxwell's riflemen were thinly posted and poured a well directed fire into the solid ranks of the advancing columns, having formed, in fact, a kind of ambuscade.

On the eighth, the American army took its position behind Red Clay creek, the left resting upon Newport on the Christiana, being on the road leading directly from the British camp to Philadelphia. The right extended a considerable distance up the creek to Hockesson. Here a battle was anticipated. But on that day, Gen. Grant having embarked the tents and heavy baggage, rejoined the remainder of the army, which was again put in motion. The main body advanced by Newark, near which they had been posted, upon the right of the American encampment and took post within four miles of that point, extending their left still further up the country. A strong column made a feint of attacking in front, and after some manœuvering, halted at Milltown, within two miles of the centre of the Americans.

This show of attacks and the simultaneous extension of the enemy's left so far up the country, indueed Washington to change his position, as he believed the object of the enemy to be to turn his right, cross the Brandywine, and cut off his communication with Philadelphia. This, if successfully carried out, would have hemmed him in upon a tongue of land between the British army and their fleet, where he must have been overpowered or compelled to fight his way out under every disadvantage.

Accordingly after reconnoitering the enemy, Washington at two o'clock in the morning of the ninth, withdrew towards Chadd's Ford, on the Brandywine, and on the evening of that day, entrenched himself upon the high ground on the left, or east bank of the creek. Maxwell's light infantry occupied the advanced posts, and during the night of the tenth, threw up defences on the right, or west bank, at the approaches to the ford.

On the evening of the ninth the British marched forward in two columns. Lieut. Gen. Knyphausen, with the left, encamped at New Garden and Kennett Square; Cornwallis with the right, occupied a piece of ground below, at Hockesson meeting house.

Early next day they united at Kennett Square, whence in the evening they advanced to within about a mile of Welsh's tavern, probably for the convenience of water.

Their army (according to Stedman,) consisted of thirty-six Hessian and British battalions, infantry, light infantry and grenadiers; a corps called the Queen's Rangers (organized, it seems, in New York) and a regiment of Light Horse. The whole were estimated at eighteen thousand men.

The column of Lord Cornwallis, on the eleventh, consisted of two battalions of grenadiers, two of light infantry, the Hessian grenadiers, part of the seventy-first regiment, and two British brigades; in all about thirteen thousand men.

That of Knyphausen consisted of two British brigades, the residue of the Hessians and Wemyss's corps of rangers; in all about five thousand.

The position of the two armies on the morning of the eleventh of September, will be seen by reference to the accompanying map. On the preceding night the British army lay at Kennett Square and to the east and west of that place, which was a small village. A road led from it directly to Chadd's Ford. Welsh's tavern (still existing) is about three miles to the east of it, on this road; a short distance beyond is Kennett meeting house and grave yard; and about a mile west of Chadd's Ford is an eminence then occupied by Maxwell's out-posts. West of Welsh's tavern a road runs directly north to the street road, and after reaching this, recommences again a short distance to the eastward, and runs again north, crossing the west branch of the Brandywine at Trimble's Ford.

Early on the morning of the eleventh the Commander-in-Chief, with the column of Cornwallis, took this road leading northwardly to Trimble's Ford, and under cover of the hills and forests, and aided by a fog, proceeded a considerable distance unobserved. Knyphausen started much later, and then pursued the direct road to Chadd's Ford, upon the eminences near which it will be remembered that Maxwell's regiment was posted. Scouting parties of light horse were also sent out upon this road.

To the east of Chadd's Ford and commanding it was posted the main body of the American army, consisting of the brigades of Muhlenburg and Weedon, forming Gen. Green's division. Wayne's division and Proctor's artillery occupied an entrenchment upon the brow of an eminence immediately above the ford. The brigades of Sullivan, Stirling and Stephens, forming the right wing, extended some distance up the river. To the left of the main body, and two miles below them, Gen. Armstrong with about a thousand Pennsylvania militia, was posted to guard Pyle's Ford.

The Fords of the Brandywine in ascending order were Pyle's Ford just mentioned; Chadd's Ford, where the attempt to force a passage was anticipated; Brinton's, one mile above and more difficult; Painter's, called also Jones's, on the street road, about three miles above Chadd's Ford, and about two and a half miles below the forks of the creek; Wister's or Shunk's, about a mile above Painter's. On the east or north branch were three fords, Buffington's, immediately above the forks, Jefferis' Ford (by mistake called

Jones's in Washington's letters and elsewhere,) about six miles from Chadd's Ford, and about a mile and a half above the forks, and Taylor's Ford about a mile and a half up higher, where "the old Lancaster Road" crossed. On the west branch was Trimble's Ford, about one mile above the forks, and full five miles from the British encampment. Seeds's Ford is unnoticed in the old annals.

The whole country abounded in forests, interspersed with plantations, more or less detached. To the east of the Brandywine it was more open, but both banks of the creek were pretty densely covered with woods. The country is undulating, the larger hills usually skirting the creek separated by flats now forming beautiful and luxuriant meadows, but then doubtless covered with the primitive forest. So dense and impenetrable were the wood and undergrowth upon these flats that a part of them above Painter's bridge on the street road bears to this day the name of Dungeon Bottom.

Birmingham meeting house is on the brow of a hill, about three miles north of Chadd's ford, one fourth of a mile south of the street road, and about two miles east of Painter's Ford.— Jones's house lies to the north, the farm extending to the street road. An orchard occupied a portion of the angle formed by the street road, and "the great Dilworthtown road," which passes both this house and Birmingham meeting house. Osborne's hill is about a mile north of the meeting house. Sconneltown (now entirely extinct,) was on the top of another eminence between Jefferis' Ford and Osborne's Hill.

"The Great Valley road," spoken of in the narratives of the battle, was the road leading from Kennett Square through Trimble's and Jefferis' Fords, and by the Turk's Head (now West Chester,) to the Great Valley, four miles north of the latter place.

Martin's tavern (now Marshalton) was about four miles west of the Turk's Head, and about two miles west of Taylor's Ford, on "the old Lancaster road," which traversed nearly the same ground upon which the Strasburg road was subsequently laid out.

Upon the roads leading to Chadd's and Taylor's Fords and towards Wilmington, parties of British light horse were sent out on the tenth, most probably to reconnoitre.

The column under Cornwallis set out at daybreak on the eleventh, that under Knyphausen, about nine o'clock. A very dense and heavy fog continued until a late hour. A scouting party of American light horse had ventured as far as Welsh's tavern, and having carelessly left their horses in front of the inn, were drinking at the bar when the advance of the British approached within a few rods, before they were discovered. The troopers fired one volley, escaped by the back of the house and fled across the fields to the woods, leaving their horses in the hands of the enemy. Tradition mentions as the only result of their fire the death of a horse belonging to one of the British cavalry, who mounted one of those left by the Americans and rode on.

About a mile beyond, the column was again fired on by a party stationed behind the walls of Old Kennett Grave Yard, and a retreating fire was kept up from behind walls and trees, until Maxwell's forces became engaged with the advance of the division. A body of troops sent to dislodge him from his position on the heights about a mile from the ford compelled him to retire until reinforced from the eminence at the edge of the creek. The front ranks of Knyphausen were then thrown into confusion, but being sustained by successive detachments, drove Maxwell back and finally across the creek. This part of the action began about ten o'clock. It is probable from the advantageous position of Maxwell's men on each side of the road and upon entrenched heights, that the loss of the British must have been considerable. Washington's Secretary, writing the same day, (before the engagement at Birmingham,) estimates their loss at three hundred killed and wounded, and adds, " ours does not exceed fifty in the whole.''

After securing the height, Knyphausen commenced a heavy cannonade, which was continued with little intermission until the ford was passed. Every feint and manœuvre was tried to present the appearance of a large force and a vehement effort to cross the ford.

Several detachments of the Americans crossed the creek and assailed the British who were labouring to throw up entrenchments and batteries. Captains Porterfield and Waggoner having thus passed over and secured a footing on the western bank, Gen. Maxwell returned in force, and a warm conflict ensued. Maxwell driving the enemy from the ground, killing thirty men, (among them a captain of the forty-ninth, and seizing some entrenching tools with which they were throwing up a battery.) The sharpness of the skirmish soon drew upon them overwhelming numbers, and the Americans were again repulsed.

Lord Cornwallis, with the larger division arrived, it may be presumed, at the summit of the hills south of Trimble's ford, before or about the time when Knyphausen moved from Kennett Square. Some cannon were discharged at this point, (and balls have been found in the vicinity,) for which it is difficult to account, unless they were designed to notify to Knyphausen their having gained a midway position, or to direct him to march to the ford.

Gen. Sullivan, who commanded the right wing of the American army, had received instructions to guard the fords as high up as Buffington's, just above the forks of the Brandywine. Scouting parties were sent out in various directions to watch the movements of the enemy. Col. Bland, with the light horse, crossed the creek at a point above the camp, probably at Painter's Ford on the street road, with orders to watch the movements of the enemy should they make any demonstrations of an attempt to turn the enemy's right. He in fact sent early information that he had seen two brigades advancing on "the valley road" towards Trimble's Ford, and that the dust appeared to rise in their rear for a considerable distance. This was confirmed by a note from Col. Ross who was in their rear, and who estimated the force that he had seen at not less than five thousand.

The intelligence being thus confirmed of a large division's being so far separated from the army at Chadd's Ford, Washington formed the bold design of crossing the Brandywine with the great body of his troops and falling upon Knyphausen, and orders were sent to Gen. Greene to cross above the ford. Before this could be effected, counter intelligence was received by Sullivan, who had advanced to meet the division under Cornwallis. This is said to have come from a major of militia, who stated that he had just left the forks, and that there was no appearance of an enemy in that quarter. It was also reported about the same time that Cornwallis had turned and was coming down the right or west bank of the creek to join Knyphausen. Sullivan communicated these reports to the Commander in Chief, and they seem to have had sufficient weight to discredit the intelligence received from Col. Bland and Col. Ross. Whether Sullivan be censurable or not for confiding in these reports, it is evident that it was within his power to ascertain the truth and that within an hour's time. The street road was open across the whole country to the westward, and the road northward led to Buffington's Ford just above the forks. Scouting parties might readily have reached Osborne's Hill, even at a late hour; but though his orders required him to guard as high up as the forks, there is every reason to believe that he had no party (except Col. Bland) on the west of the stream, north of the street road. In this all tradition concurs.

Whilst Washington was in the state of painful uncertainty produced by these conflicting accounts, Squire Cheyney rode up to the forces under Sullivan, and being uncourteously received by that General, demanded to be led to the Commander in Chief. This was done; and the earnestness of his asseverations, to the truth of which he pledged his life, secured confidence in his statements, corroborating, as they did, the earlier information of the morning. According to his account, the enemy was already at hand, and in large force, to the eastward of the creek.

The brigades of Stephen, Stirling and Sullivan, under the command of the latter were pushed forward to Birmingham meeting house, whilst Greene's division took the intermediate position that it had chiefly occupied during the day. Washington remained with the latter, holding it as a reserve in aid of either Wayne or Sullivan.

Birmingham meeting house had been for some days occupied as a hospital; probably the sick and wounded had been removed thither when the army took its position on Red Clay Creek. In consequence, the Friends had adjourned their meeting to the day of their usual meeting in the middle of the week, (Thursday,) appointing the wheelwright shop in Sconneltown as the place. On this day they met. Some time before separating, the younger members manifested uneasiness, which was fully explained, when on breaking up the meeting the whole country about Jefferis' Ford was seen covered with the British troops. The hour could have been little later than noon. Townsend, in his narrative, will be found clear and explicit as to these particulars. A heavy cannonade, the policy of Knyphausen, had been heard from below. About two o'clock in the afternoon Cornwallis's division reached Osborne's Hill, where they halted and took dinner, having marched nearly thirteen miles. Before they again fell in, the forces of the Americans were seen forming upon the brow of the opposite hill at Birmingham meeting house. Cornwallis, who with the field officers occupied the summit of Osborne's Hill, exclaimed, on seeing their movements, "the damned rebels form well."

Among the Americans, some dissention had arisen as to who should have the honour of occupying the right of their line. Gen. Deborre, a French officer, who had recently entered the service, claimed this post; and Sullivan finding that his orders upon the subject had been disobeyed, made a considerable circuit for the purpose of outreaching him, and thus was late upon the field with his brigade, and unable to form before the columns of the enemy vehemently attacked him. It would seem that Sullivan's manœuvre was unsuccessful, and that Deborre obtained the position he coveted, for Deborre's brigade was the first to give way, and the confusion evidently commenced at the extreme right of the line. This officer was suspended, and an inquiry into his conduct ordered, upon which he resigned.

The action was commenced by a party of Hessians, who crossed the street road and resting their guns upon the fence fired upon the outposts of the Americans, stationed in Jones' orchard north of his house. In half an hour, about four o'clock, the action became general.

The confusion created by the contest between Sullivan and Deborre spread through the ranks. In attempting to rally the troops, La Fayette was wounded in the left leg. Sullivan, whose own brigade was retreating, threw himself with Sterling and La Fayette personally into the conflict, and a most heroic stand was made, these officers continuing to maintain their ground until the American forces were completely broken and the enemy within twenty yards of them, when they escaped into the woods.

In the course of the day Washington had pointed out to Gen. Greene a suitable position for a second stand in the event of their being obliged to fall back from either point. As soon as the engagement at Birmingham meeting house took place, Greene quickly advanced and occupied this position. It was about a mile from Birmingham meeting house, on the road to Dilworthstown, in a narrow defile flanked on both sides by woods and commanding the road. Near this place on the road side, stood a blacksmith's shop. Here the retreating parties were stopped and formed in the rear. Several hours yet remained before the darkness of the night covered the further retreat of the Americans. Knyphausen, at the first fire at Birmingham, had attempted the passage of the ford in earnest, and after a short though severe contest, Wayne's division was compelled to abandon their artillery and retreat.

Greene succeeded in defending the pass, and maintained his position until the close of the day. The brigades of Weedon and Muhlenburg greatly distinguished themselves. The most conspicuous among them were the 10th Virginia regiment, and a Pennsylania regiment under Col. Stewart.

The entire force of the Americans could not have exceeded eleven thousand men, whilst Cornwallis's division alone is estimated at thirteen thousand. The continental troops laboured under serious disadvantages. Their muskets were not of the same calibre ; their cartridges in consequence were not adapted to universal use, and the efficacy of their fire was impaired. Many of the soldiers were raw and undisciplined troops, the more readily thrown into disorder upon being attacked whilst in motion, and before they had gained their proper position in the line.

The troops that had served during the preceding campaign proved themselves able and effective; and the fact that Sir William Howe, with the superior force under his command, after pursuing the retreating Americans but for a single mile, was then checked by a few regiments, speaks much for the valour of the continental army.

According to Howe, the loss of the British was one hundred killed and four hundred wounded, whilst that of the Americans was three hundred killed and six hundred wounded. Three or four hundred were taken prisoners, chiefly of the wounded.

The militia under Gen. Armstrong, posted at Pyle's Ford, had no opportunity of engaging.

The American army retreated during the night to Chester. The baggage had been previously sent off. Their loss of blankets was considerable, and in view of the approaching season, serious.

They had been in their knapsacks, and were mostly lost during the enagement. Seven or eight cannon and a howitzer fell into the hands of the enemy.

The ardour of the troops was unabated; and Washington immediately prepared for a second engagement.

Sir William Howe's delay is unaccountable. With the exception of some movements towards Chester and Wilmington, his army remained near the field of battle until the sixteenth, when they learned that Washington was within a short distance, at the Warren tavern on the Lancaster (or old Provincial) road in the Great Valley, and prepared to give them battle. A succession of heavy rains, which ruined their ammunition, prevented the engagement, and rendered the retreat of the Americans unavoidable.

The bold design of Washington to cross the Brandywine and attack Knyphausen, whilst Sullivan was to cross above and hold the other division in check, has, singularly enough, been the occasion of a covert attack upon his military character. The author of the Life of Gen. Greene congratulates the country upon the receipt of the false intelligence which prevented the movement, and argues that the movement would have proved injurious, as his baggage would have fallen into the hands of Cornwallis. But Washington had already removed his baggage, as is shown in his letter from Chester, dated the same evening. Nothing appears to have been more likely than that a brisk attack upon Knyphausen would have been successful in dislodging, if not completely repulsing him, and that arrangements could then have been made for the more serious conflict with Cornwallis. It is not to be supposed that Washington would have been led to follow up his advantage over Knyphausen too far, to the neglect of the more important duty of guarding the fords against Cornwallis. His caution is too well known to admit of such a supposition.

This sketch has reached its proper limit. The events which succeeded—"the Massacre of Paoli" (as it is popularly called) on the night of the 20th of September, Howe's entry into Philadelphia on the 26th, the battle of Germantown and the encampment of the Americans at Valley Forge—"the darkest hour of the Revolution," form suitable subjects for the future labours of the Society; and it is greatly to be desired that persons in the vicinity of these historial localities should engage in the work of gleaning the field of tradition that nothing may possibly be lost.

2*

# NOTICE OF THE LIFE OF JOSEPH TOWNSEND.*

Joseph Townsend was the seventh child of John and Joanna Townsend, and a grandson of Joseph Townsend, who was born in Berkshire, England, in 1686, and emigrated to this country in 1714, where he purchased and occupied a large tract of land lying in East Bradford Township, in Chester county, Pennsylvania, near which the village of West Chester is now built. Joseph, the subject of this sketch, was born on the 26th day of February, 1756, upon the original tract purchased by his grandfather. He was, by birth, a member of the religious Society of Friends, as his ancestors had been for some generations before him. He remained upon the paternal farm until 1782, and witnessed in the meantime the battle of Brandywine, which occurred on the 11th September, 1777. The devastation committed by the passage of the British army under the command of Gen. Howe, through Chester county, induced him to emigrate, and in the year 1782 he removed to the Little Falls of Gunpowder, in Harford county, Maryland, where he taught school one year. In the fall of 1783 he removed to Baltimore, and the town being then small and growing, he soon took an active part in its advancement—was a member of the Board of Health in 1794, 1797 and 1800, during the three several visitations of the yellow fever, and was active in the purchase of the Potter's Field, and the Maryland Hospital, both of which were demanded by that fatal disease. In 1794 he was one of the founders of the "Baltimore Equitable Society for Insuring Houses from Loss by Fire,"—an establishment based upon the mutual principle, and over which he presided for the long period of forty-seven years, until his death, having seen his adopted town expand into the importance of a large city, third in rank in the United States. Various other offices of trust and responsibility, he also held—both under the city and State governments, in corporate bodies, and in the administration of private estates, too numerous to mention in this short outline of his life.

He was three times married.

June 6th, 1782, to Hannah Painter, of Chester county, by whom he had two children; both of whom died.

May 31st, 1787, to Mary Matthews, of Baltimore, by whom he had eight children, one only of whom survives at this date, (a son.)

June 3d, 1803, to Esther Hallett, of Long Island, who survives him. They had a family of thirteen children, of whom five (a son and four

* The above sketch was at request kindly prepared by Henry C. Townsend Esq., a grand nephew of the author of the following narrative.

daughters) are living at this time.  Making in all a family of twenty-three, of whom but six survive, and but nine lived to years of maturity.

His brother and seven sisters, all married, and (with one exception) had families.  They remained in Chester county or removed to Philadelphia, and lived to an advanced age, from 60 to 90 years, except two sisters, who died in middle age.

Preserving the regular and temperate habits of his early life, he lived to the age of 85 years and seven months.  His death was sudden and without apparent pain.  He died in his own house in the city of Baltimore, on 5th day, 30th of the 9th month, 1841, having been arrested while at dinner, by his first death-stroke, from which he so far recovered as to rise from the table and lie down, when a second stroke, in a few moments, summoned him away from the living.

His remains were interred in Greenmount Cemetery, on First day, 10th mo. 3d, 1841.

# SOME ACCOUNT

OF

## THE BRITISH ARMY UNDER THE COMMAND OF GENERAL HOWE,

AND OF THE

## BATTLE OF BRANDYWINE,

*On the memorable 11th of September, 1777, &c. &c.*

---

During the winter of 1776 and the spring of 1777, the British army had possession of New York, Long Island, &c., and numerous were the conjectures respecting their future destiny, or on what part of the continent the ensuing campaign would be opened. This continued to be the case until the summer approached, when information was generally spread that they were making preparations to leave their winter quarters, which actually took place in the month of July, but their intended movements remained a profound secret until the latter end of the ensuing month, August, when they made their appearance in the Chesapeake Bay. It was then ascertained that their object was to get possession of Philadelphia, and to march thither the most direct and favorable route to obtain that purpose, having been led to believe that the productive country through which they were to pass would render great facilities to their contemplated march, and that but little obstruction or opposition would be met with from the inhabitants of that portion of the country. The number of soldiers under arms amounted by computation to 17,000, 5000 of them being German troops, generally termed Hessians, the former being under the command of General Howe, and the latter under General Knyphausen. The fleet conveyed them up along the mouth of the Susquehanna river, and landed them a little east of Turkey point, from which place they commenced their contemplated march. The news of their landing soon spread throughout the adjacent country, and some were of opinion that a general devastation would be the consequence. Others concluded that the country was now conquered, and peace and tranquillity would be restored by the former government's being re-established, as considerable commotion and disturbance had taken place in that section of the country respecting it.

At that time I resided at my father's, (John Townsend,) the place of my nativity, adjoining to the ground where West Chester now stands, a neighborhood where the inhabitants were alive to the prevailing reports and rumors of the day.

The first account received after their landing was, that they were at Iron Hill, a place not much known or spoken of previously as a place of note ; the next news was that they were at Allen's tavern, in the settlement of New Garden, a person having arrived who had been in sight of them, so near as to discover the buttons on their coats, which I suppose was a regiment of the German troops, who were, during the whole march, kept in front of the army, to cover the English troops from any skirmishing that might take place with the Americans, (or Rebels termed by them,) which probably would be the case before they arrived at Philadelphia, their intended winter quarters.

Things at this time began to wear a serious aspect, and the countenances of many were changed ; some of them evidently appeared gloomy, others somewhat brightened up from the consideration of pleasing prospects before them, and the favorable issue soon to be experienced.

General Washington was early apprised of the British forces' landing on the shores of the Chesapeake, and disposed of his troops in different directions to arrest their progress, in their intended march through that section of the country, and to make a stand against them at every position favorable for that purpose. A breast work was thrown up on an eminence on the east side of Brandywine creek, nearly opposite to Chadd's ford, near which his principal army was encamped. Scouting parties were reconnoitering in various directions for several miles up the said creek, to discover, if possible, the ford over which they intended to force their march.

Several persons in the neighborhood, who had manifested a disposition to support the Americans, now thought it advisable to remove their families, stock and furniture to a distance, that it might be safe from the British plunderers, as destruction would be the consequence if left in their way. Others being of a different opinion, were disposed to remain at home and risk the danger that they might be exposed to, let the consequence be what it might.

A majority of the inhabitants were of the Society of Friends, who could not consistently with their principles take any active part in the war, and who generally believed it right to remain at their dwellings, and patiently submit to whatever suffering might be their lot, and trust their all to a kind protecting Providence, who had hitherto protected and prospered their undertaking in an extraordinary manner, ever since their first settlement of the country under the proprietor and governor William Penn.

General Washington had his head quarters at Benjamin Rings'* who resided near the east side of Chadd's ford, and General La Fayette was near at hand in the neighborhood.† They were frequently together, which afforded an opportunity to spectators to view them both at the same time. Lord Stirling took possession of the dwelling of Amos House,‡ near the fording place. He was one of those who had removed his family and property to a more retired and secure place a few days previous to the army's encamping there.

On the 10th of September, in the evening, the British forces arrived and encamped at Kennett Square and its vicinity, and early on the morning following were disposed to carry into effect their concerted plan of crossing the Brandywine Creek and routing the American army from their ground of encampment, which was for General Knyphausen to conduct the troops under his command to the high grounds of the creek on the west side and commence a brisk cannonading, in order to keep up the appearance of an attempt to cross the stream of water, while General Howe conducted his troops, artillery, &c., up the creek about 7 miles to Jefferis' Ford, that he might surprise Washington's army, which lay south-east of Birmingham meeting house.

The order given to General Knyphausen was complied with. He arranged his artillery on the lands of William Harvey, Jacob Way and others adjoining, as the most eligible spot for the intended purpose, having the principal part of his troops under arms in full view of the Americans, who occupied the eminences on the east side.

General Knyphausen commenced his cannonading early after daylight, and continued it the greater part of the forenoon ; it then in a great measure ceased, and it appeared as if the troops were retiring; so much so, that a company of Americans ventured to cross the creek at the ford and advance some distance on the west side without any interruption from the enemy. Thus were the Americans amused during the forenoon, and until information arrived that General Howe and his troops were crossing the creek at Jefferis' Ford, which unexpected intelligence occasioned a

* See plan, fig. 22.    † See plan, fig. 21.    ‡ See plan, fig. 26.

general consternation and commotion throughout the whole of General Washington's army.

It may be recollected that the whole of the movements of the enemy were concealed from General Washington. He could procure no correct intelligence respecting them, except the firing of the cannon opposite Chadd's Ford. It was near 12 o'clock before the information reached him, and it took some considerable time before he could arrange his forces to risk an engagement with them, which he endeavored to do by posting such of his troops as were prepared for action, on the eminence in front of Birmingham meeting house. Some few of them were sent forward to the meeting house, the burying ground and site contiguous being favorable for the first attack, which took place accordingly.

As the object of these memoranda is to recite some particulars of the transactions of that day, I shall now turn to the early part of it, and relate some circumstances leading thereto. On the arrival of General Washington's army from the eastward, in order to impede the progress of the British, after their landing on the shores of the Chesapeake, a considerable number of the soldiers were sick in consequence of their long marches through the excessive heat of that season of the year ; on that account the commissaries and those who had the charge of the disordered persons, were obliged to take possession of the meeting houses and other public buildings as hospitals to accommodate them. Among the number thus occupied, Birmingham meeting house was to be one, and preparations were making therein for that purpose. First-day morning arrived. Friends assembled as usual, from an expectation that the meeting might be held in the house if it should be taken possession of afterwards : but from the situation of it, their request could not be granted, they therefore got permission to take some of the benches out of the house, and place them under the trees which stood in front thereof, on which they seated themselves in the quiet, as far as was practicable under existing circumstances—as the officers and workmen were moving about and engaged in making preparations to receive the sick, to be brought there as soon as the premises could be got in readiness. After the meeting had sat some time, a female Friend was concerned in public testimony—her communication was solemn and edifying. In the course of it she made mention of the visitation she had experienced when young in years from a kind Providence, who had been her support through every trial and difficulty, both inward and outward, to the present time, and the covenant she had entered into with Him to serve Him as her ability might be afforded through every dispensation she might have to pass, either within the walls of the meeting houses, or out of them, as might be her lot to experience. To me it was a favored time, and I felt thankful in being present. Under these circumstances it became necessary that some other building should be provided to accommodate the meeting in future, until the meeting house should be cleaned and put in order for the purpose, and how soon that would be the case was uncertain from the present gloomy appearance. Several houses and rooms were talked of, but it was finally concluded to hold the next meeting in a large wheelwright shop, which stood on the eminence north of the dwelling house* now owned by Philip Price, at a place called Sconnel Town. The next meeting day was on the 11th of the month, which proved to be a memorable day.

Amos House, who had left his dwelling near Chadd's Ford, and was succeeded therein by Lord Stirling and his attendants, was in the practice of visiting the premises almost daily, to see what discovery he could make, went down on the morning of the 11th, after the cannonading had commenced, and rode under the cannon balls that were discharged from the artillery on the hills on each side of the creek without receiving any injury therefrom.

Possessed of curiosity and fond of new things, my brother William Townsend and myself with some others, rode along side of the Brandywine for some distance, to discover the approach of the British army, in case they should attempt to cross any of the fords on the creek between Jefferis' and Chadd's; we fell in with many like ourselves, but no intelligence could be obtained. We then returned to the aforesaid wheelwright shop to assemble with Friends in holding our week day meeting, being near the hour appointed. While we were sitting therein some disturbance was discovered near the house and about the door, which occasioned some individuals to go out to know the cause, and they not returning, and the uneasiness not subsiding, suspicions arose that something serious was taking place, the meeting accordingly closed. On our coming out of the house, and making some inquiry of what had happened, found it to be an alarm among some of the neighboring women, that the English army was coming, and that they murdered all before them, young and old. Some of us endeavored to quiet their fears by telling them it was not likely to be the case, and that they had better compose themselves than to make further disturbance, and while we were reasoning with them, our eyes were caught on a sudden by the appearance of the army coming out of the woods into the fields belonging to Emmor Jefferis, on the west side of the creek above the fording place. In a few minutes the fields were literally covered over with them, and they were hastening towards us. Their arms and bayonets being raised, shone as bright as silver, there being a clear sky and the day exceedingly warm. Recollecting that there was no one at our dwelling, except some of our sisters, we concluded it advisable to return home as expeditiously

* See plan fig. 1.

as possible, as we had no doubt but that they were marching direct for Philadelphia, and would pass by the house and over the farm. (Our parents had a few days before been called to their daughter Lamborn's, at Kennett, on account of the illness of her children, one of whom had died during their stay there. They were considerably plundered by the rabble who accompanied the army during their encampment at Kennett Square, to which they were contiguous.)

After our arrival at home, and our horses were enclosed in the stable, we were in momentary expectation of the army's approach, but in this we were disappointed ; and having waited some time, we ventured down the roads towards them, and when in sight of Jefferis' ford, we discovered that they had turned their course towards Birmingham, and were passing by where the meeting had on that day been held. Being disposed to have a better and nearer view, we set out for the purpose, and passing by the dwelling of Abel Boake,* we soon after met Sarah, his wife, who had been as curious as ourselves, and had been among the soldiers as they marched along. The space occupied by the main body and flanking parties was near half a mile wide. She encouraged our going amongst them, at the same time admiring their appearance, and saying what fine looking fellows they were, and to use her own expression "they were something like an army," which we would see for ourselves, if we would go amongst them, and that there would not be any objection to our entrance ; thus encouraged, we walked on until we approached the flanking party, when a soldier under arms called out "where are you going ?" We replied, "we wished to see the army, &c., if there was no objection." He observed "there was their Captain, we might speak to him," which being done, leave was readily obtained, and in a few minutes we found ourselves in the midst of a crowd of military characters, rank and file: little to be discovered but staff officers, and a continued march of soldiers and occasionally a troop of horse passing ; great numbers of baggage wagons began to make their appearance, well guarded by proper officers and soldiery. We passed through them until we reached one of the most eligible houses in the town,† and soon after divers of the principal officers came in, who manifested an uncommon social disposition. They were full of their inquiries respecting the rebels, where they were to be met with, and where Mr. Washington was to be found, &c. This inquiry respecting the rebels, was a general thing among the common soldiers and others, as they moved along. The officers aforesaid, were replied to by brother William Townsend, who modestly and spiritedly told them that if they would have patience a short time, he ex-

---

* Still standing about three-quarters of a mile S. W. of West Chester, and owned by Abraham Gibbons.

† Sconneltown.

pected they would meet with General Washington and his forces, who were not far distant, (the front of his army was then in view on the heights of Birmingham meeting house, though three miles distant from us.) They inquired what sort of a man Mr. Washington was. My brother had a knowledge of him by being with him at his quarters at Chadd's Ford, and replied that he was a stately, well proportioned, fine looking man, of great ability, active, firm and resolute, of a social disposition, and was considered to be a good man. This he observed to check their ardour for a sight of him, and to bring forward some further observations from them respecting him, to which one of them answered " that he might be a good man, but he was most damnably misled to take up arms against his sovereign." During the interview, while I was conversing with one of the officers, I inquired of him at what place they had encamped the night before, to which he replied that he knew not where the main body of the army was, but their regiment lay on the south side of the hill beyond Kennett Square. He then observed to me in some rapture " you have got a hell of a fine country here, which we have found to be the case ever since we landed at the head of Elk." The house we were in was elevated, so that on the first floor where we stood we had a pretty full view of the army as they progressed along ; and while we were conversing together, my brother called on me to step to the door to see General Lord Cornwallis, who was passing by. He was on horseback, appeared tall and sat very erect. His rich scarlet clothing, loaded with gold lace, epaulets, &c., occasioned him to make a brilliant and martial appearance. The advanced part of the army made a halt at this place, and refreshed their horses by hastily cleaning off some of the corn patches that were within their lines. It may be observed that most or all of the officers who conversed with us, were of first rank, and were rather short, portly men, were well dressed and of genteel appearance, and did not look as if they had ever been exposed to any hardship : their skins being as white and delicate as is customary for females who were brought up in large cities or towns.

As we spent no idle time in viewing the strangers who surrounded us, I discovered on a sudden there was a general stir and movement among them; inquiry was made as to what could be the cause, and it was answered by one of them that they were resuming their march, and that the halt that had been made was only to refresh their horses, to enable them to perform the several duties prescribed them.

Having by this time become familiar with them, and no danger or difficulty to be apprehended from them, my curiosity or ambition was increased, and I wished a further and more full view of them than I had before had, and to have it to say that I had seen the whole of them as far as was practicable. I invited James

Johnson, an acquaintance, who was standing by, to accompany me, and we proceeded through the crowd on the public road until we reached the advanced guard, who were of the German troops. Many of them wore their beards on their upper lips, which was a novelty in that part of the country. They were then between the dwelling of Richard Strode and Osborne's Hill. Being now in the front, we walked on inconsiderately until we arrived at a pair of bars, opposite the ancient dwelling of Amos Davis,* through which we went into the field south-west! of the road, and walked up to the upper fence, being the division line between the two tracts of land of Amos Davis and the heirs of his uncle, Daniel Davis. On turning our faces back, we had a grand view of the army as they advanced over and down the south side of Osborne's Hill and the lands† of James Carter, scarce a vacant place left. While we were amusing ourselves with the wonderful curiosity before us, to our great astonishment and surprise the firing of the musketry took place; the advanced guard aforementioned having arrived at the street road, and were fired upon by a company of the Americans, who were stationed in the orchard north of Samuel Jones' brick dwelling house.‡ The attack was immediately returned by the Hessians, by their stepping up the bank of the road alongside of the orchard, making the fence as a breast work through which they fired upon the company who made the attack. From the distance we were from them (though in full view until the smoke of the firing covered them from our sight,) I was under no apprehension of danger, especially when there was such a tremendous force coming on and ready to engage in the action ; nevertheless, I concluded it best to retire, finding that my inconsiderate curiosity had prompted me to exceed the bounds of prudence. I proposed to my companion, but he refused to return, being disposed to see what further steps would take place, and how it would end.

I then made the best of my way through the crowd until I arrived at the aforementioned bars on the road, which opened into the field of Amos Davis, where I was met by several companies of soldiers, who were ordered into the field to form and prepare for the approaching engagement—the opening of the bars was not of sufficient width to admit them to pass with that expedition the emergency of the case required. A German officer on horse back ordered the fence to be taken down, and as I was near to the spot, I had to be subject to his requirings as he flourished a drawn sword over my head with others who stood by ; on the removal of the second rail, I was forcibly struck with the impropriety of being active in assisting to take the lives of my fellow beings, and therefore desisted proceeding any further in obedience to his

* See plan, fig. 5.
† Now occupied by his nephew, James Forsythe.          ‡ See plan, fig. 7.

commands. The hurry was great, and so many rushing forward under arms, I found no difficulty in retiring undiscovered, and was soon out of the reach of those called immediately into action. I lost no time on my return; and when I arrived on the top of the hill I discovered on the eminence in Samuel Osborn's field a number of my acquaintances who were standing near to a considerable number of persons on horseback and viewing them, and the different movements of the army; I joined in with them. It was now a time of some seriousness and alarm among them—the battle had commenced in earnest—little was to be heard but the firing of the musketry and the roaring of cannon from the parties. It appeared that those on horseback were some of the principal officers of the British army with their aids, who had collected together to consult respecting carrying on the engagement to the best advantage. Among them was General Howe. He was mounted on a large English horse much reduced in flesh, I suppose from their being so long confined on board the fleet between New York and the head of the Chesapeake Bay, which was about six weeks, occasioned by contrary winds, &c. The general was a large, portly man, of coarse features. He appeared to have lost his teeth, as his mouth had fallen in. As I stood alongside I had a full opportunity of viewing him as he sat on horseback, and had to observe his large legs and boots, with flourishing spurs thereon. While the officers were in consultation, and we viewing them together with the smoke issuing from the cannon and musketry, we heard a tremendous roaring of cannon, and saw the volume of smoke arising therefrom at Chadd's ford. General Knyphausen having discovered that the engagement was on with the front of Howe's army at the meeting house, he immediately forced the troops under his command across the Brandywine, and the whole of General Washington's army in that station were routed from their breastworks and the different positions which they had taken to impede the march of the British. From these circumstances General Washington concluded it prudent to effect a retreat which took place accordingly. While we remained on Osborne's hill, we had the opportunity of making many observations—the engagement of both armies—the fields in front of us containing great heaps of blankets and baggage, thrown together to relieve the men for action—the regular march of the British army, consisting of horse and foot, artillery, baggage and provision wagons, arms and ammunition, together with a host of plunderers and rabble that accompanied the army. Almost the whole face of the country around appeared to be covered and alive with those objects. Their march continued about four hours.

We remained on the hill for some time, and when the engagement appeared to be nearly over, or at least that part of it which

3*

was in view, and the day being on the decline, we were about retiring; but as admiration and curiosity had been the order of the day, I proposed to some of my companions that we should go over to the field of battle and take a view of the dead and wounded, as we might never have such another opportunity. Some of them consented, and others with some reluctance yielded. We hastened thither and awful was the scene to behold—such a number of fellow beings lying together severely wounded, and some mortally—a few dead, but a small proportion of them considering the immense quantity of powder and ball that had been discharged. It was now time for the surgeons to exert themselves, and divers of them were busily employed. Some of the doors of the meeting house were torn off and the wounded carried thereon into the house to be occupied for an hospital, instead of the American sick for which it had been repairing some days previous.

The wounded officers were first attended to—several of distinction had fallen, and as every thing appeared to be in a state of confusion, and we being spectators and assistance required, some of our number, at the request of the surgeons, became active in removing them therein—of whom I was one. I should have been willing to have been informed who they were, but it was not a time for inquiry, and I do not recollect to have heard the name of one of them mentioned at that time. After assisting in carrying two of them into the house I was disposed to see an operation performed by one of the surgeons, who was preparing to amputate a limb, by having a brass clamp or screw fitted thereon, a little above the knee joint, he had his knife in his hand, the blade of which was of a circular form, and was about to make the incision, when he recollected that it might be necessary for the wounded man to take something to support him during the operation. He mentioned to some of his attendants to give him a little wine or brandy to keep up his spirits, to which he replied, "No, doctor, it is not necessary, my spirits are up enough without it." He then observed, "that he had heard some of them say there was some water in the house, and if there was he would like a little to wet his mouth." As I was listening to the conversation and waiting for the water to arrive, one of my companions caught me by the arm and mentioned that it was necessary to go out immediately, as they were fixing the Picquet Guards, and if we did not get away in a few minutes we should have to remain within the lines of encampment during the night. I instantly complied, and we saved our distance, and were at liberty to return home.

The dusk of the evening was then on, and we set out, being twelve or fifteen in number, two of whom had started earlier and were some distance before us, and I suppose we were all under the erroneous idea that from what had passed during the day, there was not the probability of an American under arms in the whole neighbourhood. But in this we were grossly deceived, for the two persons aforesaid who had started early were talking rather freely on the defeat of the American army in the course of the afternoon, and were overheard by a scouting party which had been following the rear of the British army during the day. They were posted in a field on an eminence and viewing the movements of the British in the evening after the battle was over. They found it necessary to hail the two gentlemen, who had been and were then taking such liberties, but as no answer was returned they repeated their call, which continuing to be the case, one of them without further hesitation or ceremony fired upon them. The ball penetrated the thigh of one of them, S. K.,* and he fell.

They then rode off and were discovered travelling up the public road that led to our dwellings. The report of the musket was heard by some of our number who were behind, and that not without serious apprehensions, not knowing what it could mean. When we arrived at the place where the circumstance happened, we were informed of the particulars, and that a kind neighbour, Richard Strode, had assisted in carrying the wounded man into a small house, where he lay groaning and lamenting in a most grievous manner.

It would be difficult to express our feelings on this occasion. We were all panic struck, not knowing but what it might be our fate, or perhaps we might fare worse in a few minutes. We felt our imprudence or inconsiderate conduct with great force, and the novelties of the day were now damped. To move forward was terrifying—to remain where we were would be no small punishment under existing circumstances. Some of us had left our families, consisting only of a few females and children, and we knew not what dreadful events might have taken place in our absence. Imagination was worked up to a great height, and our fears were as great as we could bear, such was the dilemma that we were in. I considered that it had overbalanced all we had seen, and was now without remedy. A consultation was now held and we found ourselves surrounded with difficulties—to pursue the public road home was dangerous, from the expectation that the aforementioned scouting parties or others of the military were lying in wait for us, and that we might be fired upon or otherwise taken up, and carried before the prevailing power to answer for our conduct. If we attempted to return through the fields, we were apprehensive we might be met by some of the military, and more guilt would appear than if we went boldly along the road. We were two miles from home, and the moon having got up, the night was clear and bright and remarkably still, so that every movement could be discovered at a distance. After various projects being suggested, we finally resolved to take the nearest way home, which was through divers fields and woods, from a hope that there would be less danger and risque of being detected. Coming to

* Simon Kerns.

this conclusion before we set out, that no conversation should take place on the way, or observations made that would be unfavorable, provided we should be overheard. We accordingly commenced our route and reached our dwellings at a late hour of the night without molestation or alarm, except in one instance, when climbing over a fence on the way, we surprised a flock of sheep which lay alongside taking their repose—they started and ran off as if their worst enemy were in close pursuit of them. Our fears were up in an instant, not knowing but that those whom we so much dreaded were close at hand.

We found all safe and undisturbed when we arrived at home, but met with a severe reproof from one of our sisters for having taken such liberties, and given way to idle curiosity, which might have involved ourselves and family in great difficulty and distress, saying that for her part she had no wish or desire to see one person in the whole British army. I was satisfied with the correctness of her observation, but it was now too late to be remedied. I can say for myself I do not recollect ever to have felt a more thankful heart to the great Author of my existence than I did after I retired to bed, though I knew not what might be the consequences of that day's expedition when it came to be known that we had shown such an attachment to and familiarity with the enemies of our country, and which the American forces were contending against, and over whom, under the assistance of a protecting Providence, they finally prevailed, which event was the introduction and establishment of a great and powerful nation.

## APPENDIX.

Having, in the foregoing, given some account of the engagement and adventures of one day, the memorable 11th of September, 1777, I shall now proceed to give some further account of what took place shortly thereafter. The British army remained on the ground of encampment at Birmingham, until the third day of the week following, being the 16th of the month, having in the course of that time removed all their wounded that survived to the borough of Wilmington, (at that time in their possession,) amounting to 11½ wagon loads. They on that day commenced their further march for the city—having formed two divisions, one of which, commanded by General Knyphausen, proceeded by way of Chester, and the other, being the grand one under the command of General William Howe, who proceeded direct to the Swedes' ford on Schuylkill, and after marching through a severe day's rain, they encamped the following night on the south side of the valley hill and around the Boot tavern, at which house the general had his head quarters.

The ground which they had lately occupied at Birmingham

being now clear, and left in a desolate condition, exhibited a scene of destruction and waste. Some few of the inhabitants who remained thereon, and some others who were returning to their respective places of abode, found it necessary to call in the assistance of their neighbours, to re-bury many of the dead who lay exposed to the open air, and destruction of beasts and wild fowls, having (in consequence of the late heavy rains) been washed bare, and some few of them had never been interred. I was among a number who attended and performed that duty.

It would be difficult to describe the many cases of horror and destruction of human beings that came under our notice in this undertaking, but we accomplished it, though in many instances of a most disagreeable and unpleasant nature. During the performance of it, we had a full opportunity of beholding the destruction and wanton waste committed on the property of the peaceable inhabitants of the neighbourhood, and on the ground of encampment. Those who were obliged to remain thereon, had their stock of cattle destroyed for the use of the army—their houses taken away, and their household furniture, bedding, &c., wantonly wasted and burned. It was not uncommon to see heaps of feathers laying about the farms, the ticks having been stripped off and made use of, and the remains or small pieces of valuable furniture which lay about their fire places in the fields unconsumed, when there was no want of timber and fence rails that might have been used for their cooking, &c. ; but being in an enemy's country, inhabited by rebels, there was no restraint on the soldiery or rabble who accompanied them.

Having made mention that the meeting house at Birmingham had been taken out of our possession by the Americans, in order to accommodate the sick soldiers, it so turned out that before they occupied it for that purpose, General Howe had the control of it for the use of his wounded officers, and when vacated, and the army removed, Friends were at liberty to cleanse and purify, which was so far done that we held one meeting in it on the First day following after their departure, but considerable repairs were necessary afterwards, to place it in the condition it was in previous to our being deprived of it. During their occupancy of it several of the principal officers died, and were interred in the burial ground adjoining. One of them said to be a near connection of the Duke of Northumberland, a young man by the name of Percy.*

* There is a tradition that Lord Percy was killed in this battle. This is an error. Hugh Earl Percy, afterwards second Duke of Northumberland, who commanded at the battle of Lexington, and was engaged in the reduction of Fort Washington, left America previously to the battle of Brandywine, and died in England on the 10th of July, 1817, at the age of 74. See Playfair's Fam. Antiq. : 1st vol. p. 161. Gent. Mag. for July, 1817.

# SKETCH OF SQUIRE THOMAS CHEYNEY.

BY JOHN HICKMAN, JR., ESQ., OF WEST CHESTER.

The name of Thomas Cheney, familiarly known as Squire Cheyney, is connected with some of the most important incidents of the Battle of Brandywine. He has been mentioned by many of those who have written concerning that engagement, still from all that has been published, but little can be known of the true character of the man.

His parents, John and Ann Cheyney, were emigrants from England, and settled in Thornbury, Chester county. Thomas, the subject of this sketch, was their oldest child, and was born in this country, Dec. 12, 1731. There were four other children, John, Joseph, Mary and Richard. In person, Thomas was strong and athletic, with black hair, black eyes, and a complexion so dark that it was often jokingly said of him that he had been suckled by a squaw. His height was 5 feet 9 inches, and his weight 190 pounds. In character, he was an American, prudent, sagacious, resolute and brave. Through a long life his veracity was never doubted, and his honesty was proverbial. In short, he was one of those revolutionary patriots whose devotion to his country was unwavering, whose affection for it exceeded all ties of home and kindred, and whose example should be handed down to posterity as one worthy of emulation.

His father was a Friend, and his mother a Presbyterian, but his antipathy to the Friends was so very strong that he caused a burial place to be erected on his own farm, lest his ashes might commingle with theirs. He was twice married, and the father of nine children. He was living with his second wife at the time of the war. She too was on the side of her country, and like many of our grandmothers of revolutionary memory, exerted her every energy to aid her husband in all his plans.

His son Richard served in the American army, but his brothers and brother-in-law, were all in the British interest, and oft repeated and earnest were their entreaties to their elder brother to join them against the "rebels." But their entreaties, backed as they were with foreign gold, were unavailing. His course was onward, for he had made his choice. And though the land of his birth, the country of his affection, appeared on all sides in imminent danger of subjugation, yet his prophetic vision seemed to penetrate the dark and settled gloom that enshrouded it, and his heart was buoyed up with the sunny thought of "liberty and independence," feeling strong in the confidence that both alike would one day be his country's glory.

His active service in the war commenced on the day of the Battle of Brandywine. For a long time he had been watching with intense interest the movements of the conflicting armies. On this day whilst wending his way along the banks of the river, at the distance of a mile or more from Brandywine, he accidentally came upon the British army. He was ascending a high hill and when he had reached the summit, he found himself within less than an hundred yards of the enemy. They immediately pursued and fired upon him, but he rode a mare that on more than one occasion signalised herself for her fleetness, and he thus escaped. He immediately hurried to the spot occupied by Washington, and breathless with impatience, demanded access to the general. He was denied his request, but his manner became so impetuous, that it was finally granted. When admitted into the presence of Washington, he informed him that he must instantly move or he would be surrounded, that the main body of the British was coming down on the east side of the stream, and was near at hand. Washington replied, that he had received recent intelligence of their movements, and that it could not be so. Cheyney, replied, "you are mistaken general, my life for it, you are mistaken," and with great vehemence added, "by h–ll it is so, put me under guard until you find my story true." He then drew a draft of the road in the sand. Washington became satisfied, and immediately moved on to the high ground at the Meeting House, at which place they had scarcely arrived before the enemy came up. Thus the first authentic information of the direction of the British army on that day, which Washington received, was from Squire Cheyney.

The history of that hurried, unequal, and disastrous battle is familiar to all; yet it damped not the energies of Cheyney, there was fuel added to the fire in his soul that day, that urged him on with redoubled zeal. Henceforth he left all and devoted himself to the service of his country. He was ever on the alert, and by keeping the movements of the enemy in his eye, materially aided Washington by imparting to him the information thus acquired. This course he continued during all the time Washington was encamped in this section of country.

He was early suspected for a spy by the British, and as many stratagems were resorted to to entrap him, he was frequently in great jeopardy. They watched his house, and frequently entered and examined it. On one occasion, it is believed, he made his escape through the chimney. For weeks at a time he could not venture home; on such occasions he would sometimes visit a neighboring house, where his wife, patient sharer of his adversity would meet him and impart to him such information as she had acquired during his absence, and administer to him the magic cordial of deep heart felt sympathy. During a part of the winter of '78, he disguised himself as a day laborer, and in such disguise was frequently asked if he could tell where Cheyney secreted himself.

Squire Cheyney served as a Justice of the Peace before, during, and after the war; and portions of his dockets, which still exist, show that he caused many to be arrested for treason, and for carrying stores to the British army whilst in Philadelphia. A man by the name of Pennell, hired one Crossby for a bushel of salt, then an item of some value, to decoy Cheyney into the hands of the British, which he failed to accomplish, and after the termination of the war, Pennell sued him for the price of the salt before the Squire himself. It is not certainly known what his judgment was.

He was possessed of an unusual share of sound discriminating common sense, a trait of character often uncongenial to poesy—yet, like the Patriarchs of old, providence revealed to him, as by a vision of the night, the future success of his country, and poetry lent her aid in the expression of it. One night, whilst Washington was encamped at Valley Forge, suffering all the horrors of want, Cheyney had a dream. He awoke soon after, rose from his bed, and wrote it down. The paper was preserved in the family for some time, but was eventually lost. His son William having impressed it upon his memory, it was again reduced to writing with the exception of the third stanza which he could not recall. He imagined himself sitting in a strange room, near a table spread with costly articles of American manufacture, in the centre of which stood a splendid decanter filled with wine, and that after the company had seated themselves at the table, the decanter sang the following song.

1. Cheerful spirits here we'll stay
    And guard against despotic sway;
    Though Britain's numerous, frightful fleet,
    Makes ocean groan beneath its weight,
    And guns and drums cry out so loud
    To appease the vengeance of their lord,
        Yet America will be free—
        Yet America will be free!

2. Tho' vassal powers them aid afford,
    And demons crowd their council board,
    Yet Innocence will raise its cry
    And rend the cloud that shrouds the skies,
    And mercy will her aid afford,
    And confound their council board.
        Then America will be free—
        Then America will be free!

\*     \*     \*     \*     \*

4. The ruffians return in vile disgrace—
   Shame and confusion man each face,
   And when before their Lord they come
   They're struck with disappointment dumb—
   Begone ye scoundrel, paltry knaves
   You yourselves are the greater slaves,
       Since America will be free—
       Since America will be free!

Squire Cheyney lived to an advanced age. He was buried on his own farm, where his father settled when he first came to the country, about three hundreds yards north east of what is called "the shops," and within a few yards of the spot where the house stood in which he was born. There too may be seen the grave of his faithful wife, who lived to realize with him for many happy years the blessings his prophetic vision portrayed.

INSCRIPTION ON HIS TOMB.

"Sacred to the memory of
THOMAS CHEYNEY,
WHO DEPARTED THIS LIFE,
*January* 12, 1811.
Aged 79 years and 1 month."

The Cheyney property has never passed out of the family. It is now owned and occupied by Thomas W. Cheyney, a grandson of the Squire, and an inheritor of his virtues.